EXPLORING POETRY: 5 TO 8

Jan Balaam
& Brian Merrick

Photographs — Brian Merrick

ISBN 0 901291 02 1

Jan Balaam teaches at Bassetts Farm Primary School,
Exmouth, Devon

Brian Merrick teaches at the
School of Education, University of Exeter

First Published: April, 1987
Reprinted: April 1988; September,1989
July,1991; December 1995; June 1998

All of the photographs are of children at Bassetts Farm Primary School working in the
poetry lessons which were the source of this book. The captions are extracts from
the text.

Printed in Great Britain by BPC-AUP Aberdeen Limited.

CONTENTS

Thanks:

— for unflagging enthusiasm, encouragement and interest to the headmistress, staff and pupils of Bassetts Farm Primary School, Exmouth.

— for consistent help and support to Anne, Martin and Geoff.

Acknowledgements:

We would like to thank the following writers and publishers for permission to reproduce poems:

Gregory Harrison and O.U.P. for *Alone in the Grange* from 'The Night of the Wild Horses'.

Peter Young and Oliver and Boyd for *Hands* from 'Passwords I'.

Clive Sansom and Chatto and Windus for *The Train*.

Ian Serraillier and Penguin Books for *The Rescue* from 'I'll Tell You a Tale'.

Roger McGough and Penguin Books for *Bully Night* from 'Pie in the Sky'.

Karla Kuskin and Harper and Row for *The Balloon* from 'In the Middle of the Trees'.

Michael Rosen and Andre Deutsch for *Why?* from 'Wouldn't You Like to Know?'

Allan Ahlberg and Penguin Books for *Please Mrs Butler* from the collection of the same title.

Shel Silverstein and Holiday House Inc., U.S.A., for *Not Me*.

The e. e. cummings Estate and Harcourt, Brace & World Inc. for *in Just-spring* from 'Poems 1923–1954'.

The James Reeves Estate for *Cows* from 'James Reeves: Complete Poems for Children'.

We apologise for any unintentional case of copyright transgression and would like to hear from the copyright holder concerned.

INTRODUCTION

The readers we have in mind for this book are teachers and librarians—in fact anyone who might read poetry to groups of children up to the age of 7 or 8. The book grew out of five terms in which, working with two different classes, we focussed on poetry, noting the poems and activities which aroused the children most. The children were 6–7 years old.

The magic of poetry in the very early years is as strong as the magic of story; yet poetry seems to lose that power as children move into the upper years of the Primary school. The people in contact with very young children are as likely to sing a song, read a nursery rhyme, or play a game depending on rhythm and movement as they are to read a story, and any of these activities is equally likely to be requested.

In whatever circumstances a poem is encountered, it needs to be experienced rather than simply heard. A single reading may be powerful and hold the listener enthralled, but because the power within a good poem is complex and often subtle, repeated experiences bringing the listener and the poem closer together can add intensely to that initial pleasure.

It is this area which can be difficult for those uncertain about the kinds of things they might do with a poem. There is every reason to feel anxious about using a poem in ways that interfere with the experience of the poem itself, yet it may be that we can increase the enjoyment of a poem by setting it within the context of other pleasurable activities.

Our concern is to demonstrate:

— the variety of ways we have used for introducing poems to young children

— the range of activities we have used as a context in which to bring the children close to the poems following that introduction

— what seems to us a workable poetry programme for very young children.

These concerns are dealt with in the ten sections of Part I. In each of these, following a brief introduction, we give the text of the poem(s) being discussed. This is followed by suggestions under three headings which relate to different stages of experiencing a poem:

First Encounters

Developments

and

Extras

1

The 'First Encounter' for young children should be hearing it read well by someone who has personally experienced pleasure from it. A good reading will communicate the reader's pleasure. It will bring out what the reader senses is there in the words, shapes and moods of the poem. It will bring out the poem's particular qualities: effects of sound, patterns produced in the ear or on the page, humour, eeriness, and so on.

Whether you decide to develop this First Encounter will depend on the response that the poem has received. But our experience with *Cows* by James Reeves, related in the Introduction to Section 10 in Part I, indicates that a negative first response is not necessarily final.

The second stage, 'Developments', aims to link the poem to other activities the children already like. Many readers will need no advice about how to encourage discussions, set up role play, make masks, or engage in a whole range of enjoyable classroom activities. For this reason the suggestions under 'Developments' are usually stated without elaboration. Other readers may welcome some advice and for this reason Part II deals with ways of approaching each of the activities that has been suggested.

Every time you go back with a group to a poem already heard you sense how much enthusiasm the poem is arousing. When the level of enthusiasm is low it may be time to move on: a guiding principle should be *Don't labour at stirring reluctant interest*. You may, of course, think of a different approach which you feel is worth trying. This brings in another principle: *Always back your own hunches*.

When you find enthusiasm for the poem growing you may be scratching your head for more activities. This happens frequently in our experience, which is why we have included a list of 'Extras', following each basic list of Developments.

The content of each section arises from what we have done with two classes of 6–7 year olds over a period of three terms. Every activity and every poem has been 'classroom-tested'.

Each section concludes with a list of Related Poems which might lend themselves to a similar approach.

We have chosen to signal separate activities thus ★ because numbering might imply an intended sequence. Any suggestion which catches your imagination will be most effective if it is used in the context of your established practice and adapted to suit your own circumstances. Our suggestions may often work best by sparking off ideas of your own.

An initial problem may be selecting suitable poems. It needs confidence to decide what a group of children, or even one child, will enjoy. It also needs access to a range of the many collections and anthologies that are on the market.

There are two separate problems here:

— finding the poems

— deciding which poems are likely to succeed.

The first we have dealt with in Part III, where there are lists of poetry books appropriate for the early years currently available at a reasonable price. These are divided into groups, each of which could be packed in a suitable holder such as an L.P. record-case, to make a lively, varied and rich body of poems readily accessible in a classroom, or—being easily portable—shared by a number of teachers.

The second problem, deciding *which* poem, we discuss briefly in Part II where we attempt to lay down some guiding principles. We have applied these principles in the introduction to each of the ten sections in Part I where we try to answer the question:

Why choose this particular poem?

Helping and giving

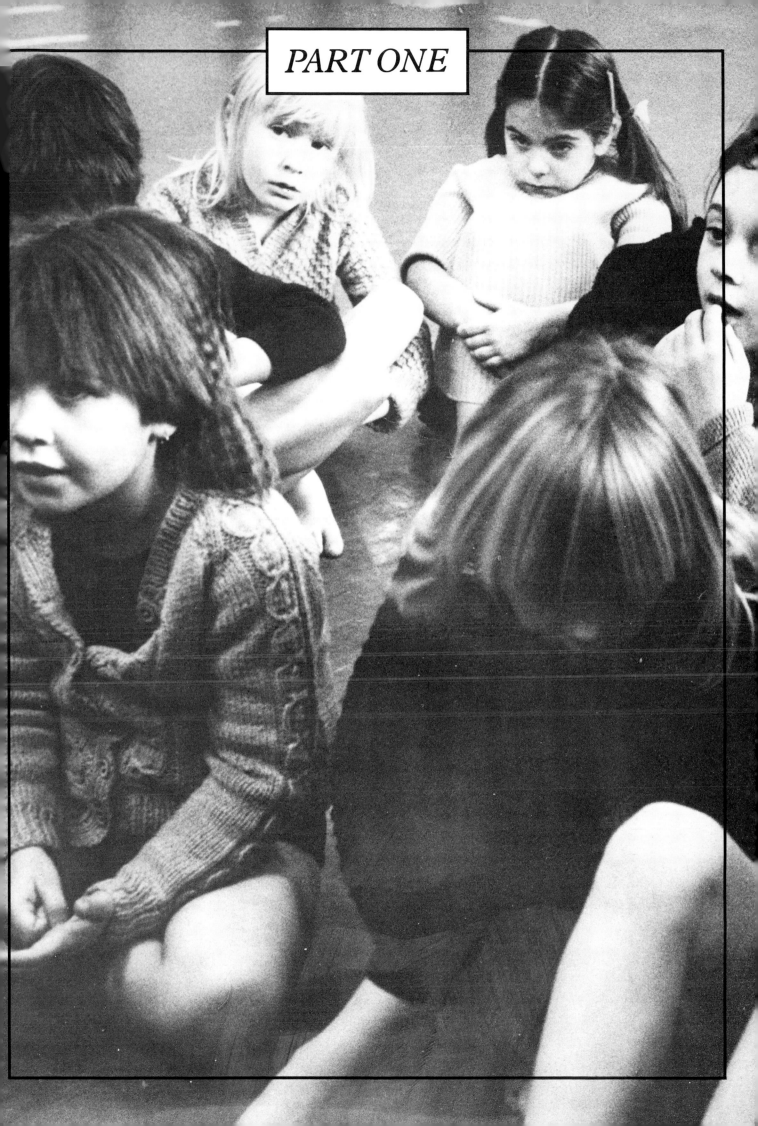

PART ONE

Imagine tapping a balloon up and down on the palm of your hand . . .

SECTION 1

Creeping up on the Grange

Very often the selection of a poem is intuitive—you are confident that a class will be roused by it on the basis of your own response and your experience of poems that *work*.

If you enjoy reading it aloud, relishing its sounds, rhythms and patterns and the vibrations that it sets up inside you, that powerfully reinforces your intuitive judgement.

'*Alone in the Grange*' comes into this category.

It works potently on the natural curiosity that we have about other people. It is a poem about their mysteriousness, their unknowableness. Whatever judgement we form of the little old man (influenced strongly, of course, by the Grange that he lives in) we can never be more sure about him than the 'I' of the poem.

Alone in the Grange

Strange,
Strange,
Is the little old man
Who lives in the Grange.
Old,
Old;
And they say that he keeps
A box full of gold.
Bowed,
Bowed,
Is his thin little back
That once was so proud.
Soft,
Soft,

Are his steps as he climbs
The stairs to the loft.
Black,
Black,
Is the old shuttered house.
Does he sleep on a sack?

They say he does magic,
That he can cast spells,
That he prowls round the garden
Listening for bells;
That he watches for strangers,
Hates every soul,
And peers with his dark eye
Through the keyhole.

I wonder, I wonder,
As I lie in my bed,
Whether he sleeps with his hat
        on his head?
Is he really magician
With altar of stone,
Or a lonely old gentleman
Left on his own?

Gregory Harrison

FIRST ENCOUNTER

★ (i) Read the poem, having tried it out several ways beforehand.

(ii) Ask the children to talk about any people they know of who live 'alone'. (In this way you will determine whether they fully understand what being alone means.) Ask the children about the people they know:

— where do they live?

— what do they look like?

— what do they do?

— how do they behave when they meet other people?

Different opinions may be voiced if more than one child knows the person being discussed.

(iii) Leave a taped version of the poem available for further listening. Use another person's voice if possible. The likelihood of them listening to it is markedly increased if the reader is someone the children recognise and relate to.

DEVELOPMENT

★ (i) The following day, or shortly afterwards, play the tape to the whole class. Join in the listening.

(ii) Discuss what the poem tells you about the little old man in the Grange. ('Grange' may need explanation.)

(iii) Ask the children for suggestions as to how more information might be collected about the little old man and his home.

Listen to these replies and be prepared to work on their suggestions.

(iv) A possible format for gathering more information through drama:

A Visit to the Grange

This can be achieved collectively in role. Let the children decide who they might be: reporters, curious townsfolk, anxious tradesmen are all obvious possibilities.

Negotiate the conditions of the drama:

— will the visit be restricted to merely observing the interior of the Grange through 'windows' or will their roles allow them to be inside?

— how will the area of the Grange be defined for them?

— will the owner be at home and if not why not?

— what signs will signal the start and end of the drama?

If the children fully understand these conditions their commitment to the drama and their involvement in it will result in the poem being explored more deeply.

(v) Interview the old man by—

(a) Teacher adopting the role of the old man. The class in role (as already decided) question him about himself and his home.

or

(b) A student-teacher, visitor or teacher, who is familiar with the poem and understands the purposes of the drama, taking on the role of the old man.

or

(c) Divide the class into groups of five or six. Ask one child to adopt the role of the old man whilst the remainder interview him.

(vi) Discuss the events of the drama with the class. Ask them to talk about what they think the old man of the poem was like.

(vii) Re-read the poem.

(viii) Ask individuals if they can supply their own answer to the final question posed by the poet.

EXTRAS

★   Let the children write down:

(a) their own description and feelings about the old man

or

(b) an imaginary page from the old man's diary.

II

or

(c) a description of a visit to the Grange.

or

(d) an account of the man written by his cook, sister, milkman, doctor etc.

★ Individuals paint or draw portraits of the owner of the Grange, according to their own view of him. These could be displayed as a portrait gallery and the label 'Lonely or Strange?' added to provoke further thoughts and comments.

★ Explore with the children the facial expressions and movements of the old man. Decide together what kind of activities are appropriate for the man, and let the children move accordingly.

RELATED POEMS

Loneliness—Janet Pomroy—in 'Junior Voices Book 1'—ed. Geoffrey Summerfield—Penguin.

Dan, the Watchman—John D. Sheridan—in 'Poems and Pictures: Night'—comp. Shona McKellar and Jan Baldwin—Evans Bros.

House—Leonard Clark—in 'A First Poetry Book'—comp. John Foster—Oxford University Press.

There was a Little Woman—traditional—in 'The Puffin Book of Nursery Rhymes'—eds. Iona and Peter Opie—Puffin.

SECTION 2

Warming and warning hitting and fitting

Many poems that become the focus of prolonged attention with the lower years are very simple. They are selected, rightly, because the teacher judges them to have particular qualities that will arouse interest and provoke response in a particular class.

The appeal of a poem may be in a single pleasing quality or combination of qualities—such as rhythm, sound, humour, familiar subject matter—which strikes a spark with the experience and inner life that the hearer brings to it. It may be a local and short-lived appeal but that in no way negates its value. If it pleases at the time, it is worth reading, and possibly following up.

The poem in this section is simple by any standards, yet it became the focus of interest with one particular class of infants over a number of sessions. It would be a logical choice for a class which has been involved in activities which require concentrated manipulative skills, such as modelling in clay or simply hand printing.

Hands

Hands
Handling
Dangling in water
Making and shaking
Slapping and clapping
Warming and warning
Hitting and fitting
Grabbing and rubbing
Peeling and feeling
Taking and breaking
Helping and giving
Lifting
Sifting sand
Hand holding
Hand

Peter Young

FIRST ENCOUNTERS

★   Read the poem to the children twice within one lesson presenting it simply as a poem you think they will enjoy.

Avoid making any comment unless questions or discussion arise from the children.

★   Two or three days later:

(i) Ask for the children's recollections of the poem. Their comments will be varied and may provide you with different ways into the poem from any that we suggest or you may have planned.

(ii) Read the poem twice more following this discussion, possibly encouraging additions to their previous comments in between the two readings.

(iii) Explore the way the sounds of some of the words in the poem reflect their meaning and the ways in which the poet makes patterns with sounds. (It is important not to lead the class to see the poem simply as a list of 'doing words'.)

★   Present the class with a reading using more than one voice. A shared reading, using another adult or child can enrich the experience of the poem. In this situation you might try the contrasting effect of reading alternate lines with splitting within a line:

Making *and shaking*

Hitting *and fitting*

You might then go on to try other divisions suggested by the children and end by establishing a preferred reading.

DEVELOPMENTS

★   (i) Ask the children to face each other in pairs and explore their partners' hands with their own. If numbers allow, join in with this activity yourself. Encourage the children to explore silently at first, using their fingers and

16

their eyes to discover small differences such as skin texture, nails and the shape of fingers, as well as the more obvious ones of size, colour and shape.

(ii) If the group shows lack of concentration or restlessness at this stage, go on to talk them through this activity by asking them to focus on specific differences and similarities as you draw attention to each in turn.

(iii) After they have explored each other's hands, gather the group together for an exchange of observations about what they have discovered.

(iv) Ask pairs to find themselves space to work on an interpretation in mime of one of the poem's couplings, such as:

— slapping and clapping

— warming and warning

— helping and giving.

You may prefer to change the earlier pairs at this stage to add variety.

Children not used to working in pairs may find it helpful to begin by working solo. The value of eventually pairing lies in the shared ideas and the sense of co-operation that may result. Whether you select the couplings from the poem yourself or leave the children to select their own will depend on how used they are to working in this way. If you feel they can select their own you will need to read the poem again at this point to remind them of alternatives.

(v) Eventually some or all of these mimes may be shown to the full group and comments invited from the observers, so demonstrating that the teacher's comments are not the only ones that are valued and valid.

★ (i) Prepare group readings with a minimum of teacher help. This follows on best from a preliminary period when children have had opportunities to become more familiar with the poem by trying their own readings, recording them and listening to other taped versions (including the teacher's).

(ii) If the group still shows interest in the poem and is capable of the necessary commitment and concentration, try working towards a larger group interpretation of the poem to be accompanied by one of the readings.

★ (i) Encourage the children to think up new word pairings associated with hands, feet, eyes, or other parts of the body.

17

(ii) Combine these words to produce individual or group poems, leading to final drafts written out on the appropriate shape. (Older infants might enjoy writing their own poems about hands or a similar subject, but creating a word pattern of their own.)

RELATED POEMS

Finger Rhymes (*Chop-chop*, *Mix a Pancake*, etc)—in 'This Little Puffin'—comp. Elizabeth Matterson—Puffin.

I Live in the City—Anon.—in 'A Third Poetry Book'—comp. John Foster—Oxford University Press.

Going Barefoot—Judith Thurman—in 'A First Poetry Book'—comp. John Foster—Oxford University Press.

My hands have been working—P. Spratt, and *Mind*—Polly Chase Boyden—in 'Ourselves: Poems and Pictures'—comp. Shona McKellar and Jan Baldwin—Evans Bros.

Group poster by three 6–7 year olds to illustrate OVERHEARD ON A SALTMARSH.

The children explained: The nymph is red. The nymph is painted off the ground because she is a good jumper, which explains how she stole the beads from the moon. The goblin is a good runner. The background is painted black because it makes the picture more frightening.

The strongest reason for choosing a poem for a class is that it is a personal favourite which you have cherished since your own childhood. The poem in this section is in this category for both of us.

It is an overheard conversation between two characters—a nymph and a goblin. The conflict in the poem is familiar but it takes place in an elemental world, inhabited by men, but where nymphs and goblins live among reeds and mud and water in close communion with the wind and the stars and the moon.

Overheard on a Saltmarsh

Nymph, nymph, what are your beads?
Green glass, goblin. Why do you stare at them?
Give them me.

       No.

Give them me. Give them me.

       No.

Then I will howl all night in the reeds,
Lie in the mud and howl for them.
Goblin, why do you love them so?
They are better than stars or water,
Better than voices of winds that sing,
Better than any man's fair daughter,
Your green glass beads on a silver ring.
Hush, I stole them out of the moon.
Give me your beads, I desire them.

       No.

I will howl in a deep lagoon
For your green glass beads, I love them so.
Give them me. Give them.

       No.

Harold Monro

FIRST ENCOUNTERS

★ (i) Read the poem to the class, making a clear distinction between the two voices.

Ask who the two speakers are in the poem. (Try to avoid reading a version which has an accompanying illustration.)

(ii) Read the poem a second time, preferably with another voice—adult or child—reading one of the parts. It will be useful to have this version on tape.

(iii) Ask for first impressions. If necessary raise some points for discussion:

— what sort of conversation are the speakers (people?) in the poem having?

— how do you think they feel about each other?

— why does the goblin want the beads?

— how do you think the nymph obtained the beads?

★ Make copies of the poem available alongside your taped version.
Suggest that children work in pairs to prepare their own reading.
(Enthusiastic non-readers might learn it for presentation to the rest of the class.)

DEVELOPMENTS

★ (i) Explore the word 'No' since it appears so frequently in this poem.
Working in a circle encourage the children to try saying 'No' in turn.
Some groups may need talking through this activity: how would you say 'No' if . . .

— you were very cross?

— you were considering changing your mind?

— you were frightened?

(ii) Let the children try saying 'No' accompanied by any body movements they feel are appropriate, such as shaking fists, folding arms, stamping feet. Where possible let suggestions come from them but be prepared with some of your own to start them off.

22

(iii) Read the poem again. Ask the children to work in pairs on a mime to accompany a reading of the poem.

Allow time for pairs to show their mimes to others and encourage comments.

★ Let the children assume the role of a nymph or goblin, (but *not* one of the actual pair within the poem), whilst you assume the role of an authority over them (for example, a Lord or Queen).

In this role you may all explore some of the questions raised by the poem and help individuals to clarify anything that reading the poem has left vague.

Becoming a nymph or goblin takes them nearer to an understanding of how they might feel if they were involved in the argument central to the poem.

★ Explore the children's visual impressions of the poem's characters.

Provide various materials, such as paint, pens, crayons, coloured paper, pastels, and ask the children to show you how the goblin or nymph appears to them.

They might work individually or in groups of 3 or 4.

Those in groups should work by group decisions to produce a large picture depicting both goblin and nymph. This will necessitate children talking through their own ideas and listening to others in order to obtain a group interpretation.

The result of this activity should be a gallery of mythical characters which will be a source of further comment and questioning.

EXTRAS

★ In pairs children:

(a) Reconstruct the argument within the poem but expand it to include their own ideas, such as:

— can the goblin offer reasons for wanting the beads which will change the response of the nymph?

— can the nymph find ways to discourage the goblin from desiring the beads?

or

(b) (i) Act out real or imaginary arguments arising from the children's own experiences of desperately wanting something they could not have.

(ii) Discuss arguments in general: why they start, how the children feel about them, how they are resolved.

★ Prepare your own simple prose version of the story told within the poem (though some children may enjoy doing this for themselves).

The children then individually write what happened next. In other words they find their own solution to the argument between the nymph and the goblin.

The results of this can be put together to provide *The Book of the Nymph and the Goblin* to be read and enjoyed again and again.

RELATED POEMS

Figgie Hobbin, 'Quack!' said the Billy Goat, and *A Fox Came into my Garden*—Charles Causley—in 'Figgie Hobbin'—Puffin.

Tweedle-Dum and Tweedle-Dee—Lewis Carroll—in 'Through the Looking Glass'—various.

Taffy was a Welshman—traditional—in 'Old Fashioned Nursery Rhymes'—comp. Jennifer Mulherin—Granada Dragon.

I'm the youngest in our house and *Last one into bed*—Michael Rosen—in 'You Can't Catch Me'—Michael Rosen and Quentin Blake—Andre Deutsch.

SECTION 4

Try combining body
beats and the words

In the forefront of our minds when we select poems for very young children are the natural impulses on which the poem might work. Amongst these is the common impulse to react positively to rhythm and expressive sound. At this stage children often respond to particular words and patterns of words with delight—yet the words seem to communicate through sound and context rather than through a previously formed meaning.

This section focusses on a poem which delights through the play it makes with one familiar pattern of sound—a train running along rails. Confronted with 'jicketty-can' the audience needs no telling that this represents the sound of the train although they have never encountered these words before. The sound and the context are sufficient.

All of the activities suggested in connection with the poem centre on the fact that it is a joy to read and a joy to hear read.

The Train

The train goes running along the line
Jicketty-can, jicketty-can.
I wish it were mine, I wish it were mine.
Jicketty-can, jicketty-can.
The engine driver stands in front,
He makes it run, he makes it shunt;

Out of the town,
Out of the town,
Over the hill,
Over the down,
Under the bridge,
Across the lea,
Over the ridge
And down to the sea,
With a jicketty-can, jicketty-can,
Jicketty-jicketty-jicketty can,
Jicketty-can, jicketty-can.

Clive Sansom

FIRST ENCOUNTER

★ (i) Before reading the poem, or after the first reading, discuss train journeys with your group. Some children's experiences may differ considerably from others. Where possible use the children's own anecdotes and pictures to build up a scene.

(ii) Read the poem, making sure that variations of pace and rhythms are brought out in your voice.

(iii) Observe the children's reaction to the poem and listen to their comments.

(iv) Read the poem again.
Ask them to comment on the way the poem was read and to suggest possible variations.

DEVELOPMENTS

★ Taking the words 'jicketty-can' try all or some of the following (sitting in a circle helps the children to know clearly when it is their turn to join in):

— each child says 'jicketty-can' in turn, trying to keep a consistent rhythm.

— go round the circle again, but this time each child tries varying the volume and/or speed of the words. (Young children will enjoy making their sound train leave a station slowly and build up speed, only to slow down at another station.)

— staying with the rhythm of 'jicketty-can': clap it, stamp it, and generally improvise with various body beats.

— try combining body beats and the words. This can be done individually or in groups, depending on the age and ability of the class.

— read the poem again, with the children adding a soft tapping accompaniment. The accompanying rhythm might be provided by constant repetition of the words 'jicketty-can'.

★ Make a tape available to the class on which you have recorded your own voice repeating 'jicketty-can' using variations of speed and volume.
Suggest individuals or pairs invent other word patterns to fit the rhythm and tape them after yours. (Children may have played this game on a train journey before.)

As far as possible, leave the children to experiment in this way on their own.

When you feel the children have had enough time to contribute to the tape (which might be some days later) put aside a short session for you all to listen to it.

The children will have fun identifying their own rhythms and listening to others.

★ From the tape write down some of the word patterns. Put these on large cards and add them to a music corner where children may explore them further with the aid of both tuned and un-tuned instruments.

★ Provide copies of the poem for children to work on their own readings, possibly with pairs combining—one to provide a reading and the other to provide a suitable rhythmic background.

Alternatively small groups could work on a rhythmic background to accompany you while you read the poem.

EXTRA

★ Prepare the poem with a backing for an audience, such as another class or a visiting adult.

Working towards a final presentation of this kind provides children with a clear objective and a sense of occasion, which not only produces a more committed end product but serves to hold the poem for the child in a concrete memory.

This may also lead to a final recording to be replayed, enjoyed and recalled at any time.

RELATED POEMS

The Picketty Fence—David McCord—in 'Days Are Where We Live and Other Poems'—comp. Jill Bennett—Bodley Head.

The Song the Train Sang—Neil Adams—in 'Poems for Seven Year Olds and Under'—comp. Helen Nicoll—Young Puffin.

From a Railway Carriage—R. L. Stevenson—in 'A Child's Garden of Verses'—various.

Billy's Bath—Clive Riche—in 'A Very First Poetry Book'—comp. John Foster—Oxford University Press.

Bonking All the Drains—Michael Rosen—in 'Quick, Let's Get Out of Here'—Puffin.

Building Site—Marian Lines—in 'A First Poetry Book'—comp. John Foster—Oxford University Press.

Tailor—Eleanor Farjeon—in 'A Puffin Quartet of Poets'—Puffin.

One Misty Moisty Morning—Anon—in 'A Puffin Book of Nursery Rhymes'—comp. Iona and Peter Opie—Puffin.

Taffy was a Welshman—Anon—in 'Old Fashioned Nursery Rhymes'—comp. Jennifer Mulherin—Granada Dragon.

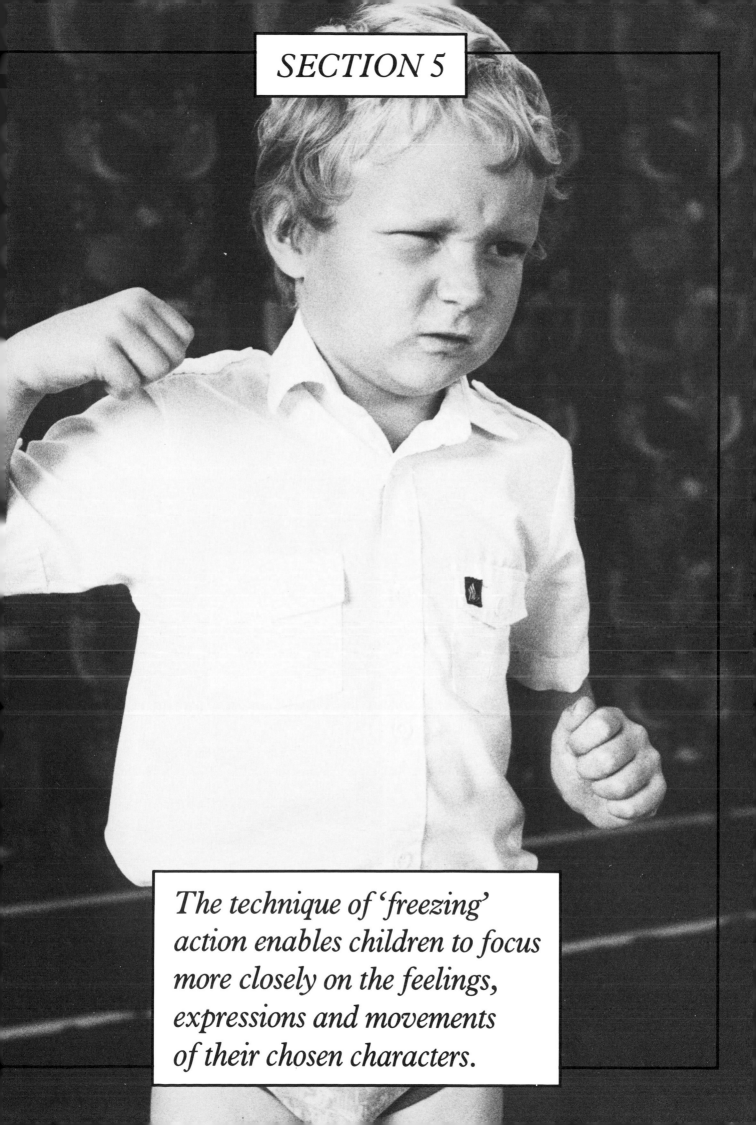

The technique of 'freezing' action enables children to focus more closely on the feelings, expressions and movements of their chosen characters.

Charles Causley, writing about the poems in his collection, 'The Puffin Book of Magic Verse', says:

> 'A poem is not an object, fixed in space and time, with a single, immovable meaning. It is a living organism which we can study, match with our own experience of life, and of which we may make something new every day.'

Amongst the poems we chose to work with, the poem in Section 5 illustrated this statement forcefully.

We chose it without any particular excitement or sense of it being special: it was one of many we selected because we thought the class would enjoy its subject matter.

Their response was immediate and startling. The wide variety of suggestions that follow about ways of enjoying and savouring the poem are also a record of what we did as the class clamoured to hear it and talk about it again and again.

There were frequent signs that, for them, this was 'a living organism' and that they were making something new of it at each encounter.

The Rescue

The wind is loud
The wind is blowing,
The waves are big,
The waves are growing.
What's that? What's that?
A dog is crying,
It's in the sea,
A dog is crying.
His or hers
Or yours or mine?
A dog is crying,
A dog is crying.

Is no one there?
A boat is going,
The waves are big,
A man is rowing,
The waves are big,
The waves are growing.
Where's the dog?
It isn't crying.
His or hers
Or yours or mine?
Is it dying?
Is it dying?

The wind is loud,
The wind is blowing,
The waves are big,
The waves are growing.
Where's the boat?
It's upside down.
And where's the dog,
And must it drown?
His or hers
Or yours or mine?
O, must it drown?
O, must it drown?

Where's the man?
He's on the sand,
So tired and wet
He cannot stand.
And where's the dog?
It's in his hand,
He lays it down
Upon the sand.
His or hers
Or yours or mine?
The dog is mine,
The dog is mine!

So tired and wet
And still it lies.
I stroke its head,
It opens its eyes,
It wags its tail,
So tired and wet.
I call its name,
For it's my pet,
Not his or hers
Or yours, but mine—
And up it gets,
And up it gets!

Ian Serraillier

33

FIRST ENCOUNTERS

★ Read the poem in isolation or with others (see 'Related Poems').

The reading should make the most of the atmosphere and sense of suspense the poem evokes. The poem does not require more than one reader but another reader's interpretation might provide contrast. Male and female voices could heighten this.

Allow plenty of time after the first reading—anything from half a day to a week—for the impact of the poem to be absorbed.

★ (i) Read the poem again or listen to a taped version of it.

(ii) If there are no spontaneous comments start by asking questions, such as:

— where do you think the owner was whilst the dog was in the sea?

— how did the dog get into the sea?

— at what point in the poem did you think the dog was either going to die or to survive?

— what feeling(s) did the end of the poem leave you with?

At this stage children may want to tell about other rescues more personal to them which have left a lasting impression.

DEVELOPMENTS

★ Have a colleague, student-teacher or helper visit the class in role as the boatman involved in the rescue. (The addition of suitable clothes will add to the children's belief in the role-play.)

Let the children ask him questions about the events which were briefly described in the poem.

If the children have had little experience of role play you could prepare them for the visit by explaining what is to happen and allowing them to assume their own roles as bystanders, reporters or whatever seems appropriate. Time might be spent thinking up suitable questions to ask in order to start the ball rolling.

In the absence of an available 'boatman' you might assume the role yourself, though this would interfere with your detached enjoyment of the children's reactions.

★ Out of role, discuss the boatman and what they discovered whilst talking to him. Ask the children what sort of person they considered him to be.

34

Up to now it is probable that most of the children will have been more concerned with the dog than the boatman. This discussion should help them explore their attitudes towards the rescuer in the poem.

★ Within a week of the first reading, read the poem again.

Ask the children who might have seen the rescue.

Build up groups of bystanders likely to be seen on or near the sea-shore. (Use the children's suggestions.) Discuss their activities then create a series of still photographs of three scenes on the beach: *before, during* and *after* the rescue. The changes from still scene to still scene might accompany a reading of the poem.

The technique of 'freezing' action enables children to focus more closely on the feelings, expressions and movements of their chosen characters. Afterwards the children can talk about what their characters were feeling and thinking. (The credibility of the action—and ultimately the poem—will more than likely be marred if any child assumes the role of the dog!)

★ Repeat the previous activity but let half the class observe whilst the others perform, then reverse the procedure. This will provide an audience for the action and enable each group to comment and make suggestions which may in turn sharpen their own interpretations.

★ Individuals or pairs paint a sea wash. Fingers and/or sponges may be used to produce varied effects. When the background is dry details of the dog, rescuer, boat and the dog's owner can be added. Coloured inks or charcoal make an interesting contrast to the background but children may have suggestions of their own. Decisions will have to be made as to what the characters will be doing and where they will be positioned in relationship to each other.

When complete these pictures may be displayed and discussed. By listening to the poem again or by reading it themselves children may select an appropriate line or lines from the poem which can be written as a caption to place below the picture.

★ When the group is familiar with the poem—say after they have heard it four or five times—they may enjoy listing, with your help, the sounds mentioned in the poem: such as the wind, the waves, the dog crying. Some children might then try producing these background noises vocally or with the use of musical instruments to accompany a reading of the poem.

35

EXTRAS

★ Individual children might:

(a) Write a report of the rescue for an imaginary newspaper.

(b) Write a letter as though they were the dog's owner thanking the boatman for his help.

Small Groups might:

(c) Devise their own plays about the rescue. These might be presented to another class.

(d) Prepare a reading of the poem, possibly with sound effects (see above), which may also be presented to another class.

(e) Improvise a conversation between the dog's owner and the boatman after the rescue.

Pairs might:

(f) Divide into A and B. A tells B what happened on the beach at the time of the rescue. B questions A about what she or he does not understand.

★ Finally, talk about 'being brave':

What does it mean? Was anyone in the poem brave? If so, who?

RELATED POEMS

The Sea—James Reeves—and *The Tale of Three Landlubbers*—Ian Serraillier—in 'A Puffin Quarter of Poets'—ed. Eleanor Graham—Puffin.

The Rescue—Geoffrey Summerfield—in 'Welcome and Other Poems'—Andre Deutsch.

And it was Windy Weather—James Stephens—in 'Wordscapes'—comp. Barry Maybury—Oxford University Press.

The wind has such a rainy sound and *The Houses of the Sea*—Christina Rossetti—in 'Sing-Song: A Nursery Rhyme Book' (1872)—reprinted by Dover Publications.

Boasting and *A Girl Calling*—Eleanor Farjeon—in 'Invitation to a Mouse'—Knight Books.

The Rogery Birds—Mary Gilmore—in 'The Puffin Book of Magic Verse'—chosen by Charles Causley—Puffin.

*The masks can be simple
or elaborate, as you choose . . .*

Mister Fox

A fox went out in a hungry plight,
And he begged of the moon to give him light,
For he'd many miles to trot that night,
  Before he could reach his den O!

And first he came to a farmer's yard,
Where the ducks and geese declared it hard
That their nerves should be shaken and their rest be marr'd,
  By the visit of Mister Fox O!

He took the grey goose by the sleeve;
Says he, 'Madam Goose, and by your leave,
I'll take you away without reprieve,
  And carry you home to my den O!'

He seized the black duck by the neck,
And swung *her* over across his back;
The black duck cried out, 'Quack! Quack! Quack!'
  With her legs hanging dangling down O!

Then old *Mrs.* Slipper-Slopper jump'd out of bed,
And out of the window she popp'd her head,
Crying, 'John, John, John, the grey goose is gone,
  And the fox is away to his den O!'

Then John he *went up* to the top of the hill,
And he *blew a blast* both loud and shrill;
Says the fox, 'That is very pretty music—still
  I'd rather be in my den O!'

At last the fox *got home to his den;*
To his dear little foxes, eight, nine, ten,
Says he, 'You're in luck, here's a good fat duck,
  With her legs hanging dangling down O!'

He then sat down with his hungry wife;
They did very well without fork or knife;
They'd never ate better in all their life,
  And the little ones pick'd the bones O!

Anon.

A Fox Jumped Up One Winter's Night

A fox jumped up one winter's night,
And begged the moon to give him light,
For he'd many miles to trot that night
Before he reached his den O!
Den O! den O!
For he'd many miles to trot that night
Before he reached his den O!

The first place he came to was a farmer's yard,
Where the ducks and the geese declared it hard
That their nerves should be shaken and their rest so marred
By a visit from Mr Fox O!
Fox O! Fox O!
That their nerves should be shaken and their rest so marred
By a visit from Mr Fox O!

He took the grey goose by the neck
And swung *him* right across his back;
The grey goose cried out Quack, quack, quack,
With his legs hanging dangling down O!
Down O! down O!
The grey goose cried out Quack, quack, quack,
With his legs hanging dangling down O!

Old *Mother* Slipper-Slopper jumped out of bed,
And out of the window she popped her head;
Oh! John, John, John the grey goose is gone,
And the fox is off to his den O!
Den O! den O!
Oh! John, John, John, the grey goose is gone,
And the fox is off to his den O!

John *ran up* to the top of the hill,
And *blew his whistle* loud and shrill;
Said the fox, That is very pretty music; still—
I'd rather be in my den O!
Den O! den O!
Said the fox, That is very pretty music; still—
I'd rather be in my den O!

The fox *went back to his hungry den,*
And his dear little foxes, eight, nine, ten;
Quoth they, Good daddy, you must go there again,
If you bring such good cheer from the farm O!
Farm O! farm O!
Quoth they, Good daddy, you must go there again,
If you bring such good cheer from the farm O!

The fox and his wife, without any strife,
Said *they never ate a better goose* in all their life;
They did very well without fork or knife,
And the little ones picked the bones O!
Bones O! bones O!
They did very well without fork or knife,
And the little ones picked the bones O!

Anon   39

Ballads belong to a rich body of literature which has its roots in story telling and song around the family hearth or tribal fire. Because they were known widely before they were ever printed, many of the ballads which move us powerfully to-day exist in a variety of forms.

Some of the differences lie in the metrical structures. Others are differences of detail and stages in the story. Such differences are often regional and arise from modifications made by individual tellers adapting their material to satisfy the needs or the tastes of the community they were addressing. But invariably the differences are slight and the common root of the various versions is obvious.

The early tellers or singers of ballads catered for whole communities and their audiences included all from the youngest to the oldest members. For this reason many ballads work potently in the minds and imaginations of young children. Because they depended on oral transmission, each ballad has qualities which make for easy remembering: strong rhythm and metrical pattern, strong and regular rhyme, a stark simplicity of detail and characterisation, frequent repetition of words, lines or chorus, and snatches of dramatic dialogue. The same qualities that make for easy remembering make for compelling listening.

The two versions of the ballad given in this section demonstrate many of these qualities and contrasts. We have drawn your attention to some significant or particularly interesting changes by the use of italics. Most of the suggestions that follow assume that the teacher will select one version rather than switch from one to the other.

FIRST ENCOUNTER

★ (i) Read the poem. If other adults are available they might read the lines spoken by the fox, Mrs. Slipper-Slopper, and the babies, and the 'quack, quack, quack' of the victim.

(ii) Ask the children what words they would use to describe the poem. They may offer words such as *cruel, sad, like a song* or even *long*. They may notice that the poem tells a story.

(iii) Ask the children to concentrate on the pictures that form in their minds as you read the poem a second time. They may do this more easily if they close their eyes.

(iv) Ask individuals to describe pictures conjured up for them. Encourage them to give as much detail as possible.

(Listening to each other's descriptions will reveal how other children's perceptions contrast with their own.)

DEVELOPMENTS

★ (i) Make a list with the class of all the characters who appear in the poem. Taking each character in turn discover what the poem actually tells us about them, then ask the children to build on these brief descriptions by adding their own ideas.

The poem, for example, tells us the fox has a wife and ten children, but what does the fox look like? Is he lean and hungry or fat and greedy?

Who do they think John might be?

What do they think Mrs. Slipper-Slopper looks like and why is she called by that name?

(ii) Provide a basic shape for children to make masks to represent all of the poem's characters. Should you wish the whole class to be involved numerous duck and goose masks might be produced and maybe other farm animals too. The masks can be as simple or elaborate as you choose—depending on the needs, age range and ability of the group. Furry fabrics and feathers can be used, but paint, tissue or paper fur and feathers make attractive alternatives. The addition of a coat of varnish both enhances the finished mask and lengthens its life.

★ (i) In the largest space you can provide explore the movements associated with the poem's characters, both animal and human.

Encourage the children to give words to describe how each might move.

If necessary pose some problems:

— how might the fox move: *on his way to the farm? on his way home?* What accounts for the difference?

— what might the ducks and geese be doing in the farmyard: *before the arrival of the fox? after the arrival of the fox?*

(Remember that it is not necessary for children to walk on all fours when assuming the role of an animal. More concentrated and thoughtful movement may be achieved by remaining upright.)

(ii) Explore the poem's characters and their movements whilst wearing the appropriate masks.

Discuss with the class the difference that wearing a mask makes.

Give them the opportunity to observe others working and to comment on the appropriateness and quality of their movements.

(iii) From the children's ideas and suggestions build up a sequence of events as described in the poem to form a short play.

The play may be a mime to accompany a reading of the poem with the key characters speaking their own lines. Alternatively the children might improvise a dialogue telling the story within the poem in their own words. Whichever way your class chooses to present it, providing an audience will give a goal to work towards and add a sense of occasion to the final performance.

EXTRAS

★ Make a book retelling the story of the fox and the duck using the children's illustrations and either the children's own words or the appropriate lines from the poem.

★ Ask the children to retell the story in their own words embellishing it with their own ideas. This might be done by one child starting, other children adding bits, and so on until the story is told.

★ Read some other version(s) of the poem. Children may enjoy spotting similarities and differences and selecting a personal favourite. Alternatively, different versions might be recorded onto tape and copies of the different versions displayed in the classroom.

★ Pose the question: Do you feel angry with the fox at the end of the poem or not? (In our case, an impassioned discussion resulted.)

RELATED POEMS

A frog he would a-wooing go—Anon—in 'Old Fashioned Nursery Rhymes'—comp. Jennifer Mulherin—Granada Dragon.

One for the Pot—Anon—and *The Frog and the Crow*—Anon—in 'The Puffin Book of Nursery Rhymes'—comp. Iona and Peter Opie—Puffin.

Gabble-Gabble—James Reeves—in 'A First Poetry Book'—comp. John Foster—Oxford University Press.

The Owl and the Pussy-Cat—Edward Lear—in 'The Oxford Book of Children's Verse'—comp. Edward Blishen—Oxford University Press.

. . . individual portraits of how the balloon-man might look.

At night I feel scared because once I had a bad dream about an elephant and I keep thinking that the elephant is going to poke his trunk through the window and snatch me and take me away. and Sometimes the shadows of my toys make scarey shapes.

by poul collins.

... *some honest sharing of anxieties* ...

The poem in this section appealed initially because of its subject matter—an experience common to everyone in the class, and deeply disturbing to many of them.

It appealed even more because of the power of the central image, and the sharp focus the poem gives to those details of the experience that make it disturbing: all of this in terms to which even very young children might respond.

Finally it appealed because of its structure—particularly the repetition in the last verse which leads so intriguingly to a suspended ending.

An unexpected bonus in reading it with the class was the ease with which it led into some honest sharing of very real anxieties and some frank insights into common blurrings of the imaginary and the real.

Bully Night

Bully night
I do not like
the company you keep
The burglars and the bogeymen
who slink
while others sleep

Bully night
I do not like
the noises that you make
The creaking and the shrieking
that keep me
fast awake.

Bully night
I do not like
the loneliness you bring
the loneliness you bring
The loneliness, the loneliness
the loneliness you bring,
the loneliness you bring
the loneliness, the

Roger McGough

47

FIRST ENCOUNTERS

★ (i) Read the poem amongst two or three poems with a similar theme (see end of section: *Related Poems*).

Later in the same day read the poem in isolation. We found that the final verse needed particularly careful preparation.

(ii) Ask for the children's first reactions to the poem. Talk through their ideas of a 'bogeyman' as this may be an unfamiliar term.

(iii) Go on to talk about burglars if this has not already arisen. Their opinions will necessarily be influenced by the burglars they may have met through television, films and stories.

(iv) Repeat your reading of the poem.

★ (i) Explore through movement the way a burglar might look and move at night when 'working'.

Allow time for children to observe and comment on others' movement. Encourage close observation and thoughtful comment.

If children find this difficult ask them:

—why do burglars have to move quietly?

—why do they need to look out for others?

—what might they carry?

—how might they feel?

—how would their *feelings* show in their faces? Their movement?

(ii) In the same way explore through movement the way a bogeyman might move, look and act. Once more encourage them to question their own and others' movements and ideas.

(iii) Draw the class around you to exchange views on the similarities and differences between burglars and bogeymen. Do they fear one more than the other? Why?

(iv) Re-read the poem.

48

★ (i) Shortly after this session, but preferably on the same day, let the children illustrate one or both or the two characters explored through movement.

Paint, collage materials and charcoal need to be available so that individuals may make suitable choices to convey their personal impressions.

(ii) With individual children, discuss the reasons for their choice. Some may deliberately choose not to make their character appear frightening and this could be a matter for further discussion.

(iii) Display the illustrations. They may provide a starting point for further talk and will hold the poem in the minds of the children.

★ (i) The following day re-read the middle verse of the poem and try all or some of the following:

(a) As a class discuss and draw up a list of noises that they hear at night when in bed.

(b) Working individually, make separate lists of non-frightening and frightening sounds. (The categories may vary from child to child.)

(c) Working in twos or fours produce some night noises. These can be created with their own voices, or by using musical instruments or everyday objects.

(d) In the same groups record a set of night noises. Other children can listen to these later and try to identify the sounds.

(e) In a circle individuals select one sound, such as a clock ticking, an owl hooting, a baby crying, and produce the sound one after the other, proceeding around the circle until each child has participated. (This is probably enjoyed even more when repeated—several times if necessary—with a positive aim of clarifying, simplifying and 'sharpening' the sound.)

EXTRAS

★ (i) Ask the children to close their eyes and listen to any sound they can hear

(a) in the classroom

(b) outside the classroom but still in the school

(c) outside the school

49

Give at least two minutes for each one. Compare what they heard in each case.

(ii) *Either* ask them to imagine what they would have heard if they had been listening in their bedroom at night and write about it.
Or ask them to make a point of listening in the same three ways in bed that night so that they can talk and write about what they heard the next day.

★ Write about Bogeymen within a 'bogeyman' shape which each one draws and cuts out for him/herself. They might group what they write according to some connection:

    — what the bogeyman looks like—his face—body—arms—how big he is

    — what noise he makes—what kind of clothes or coat he has—what he carries—what he likes doing

    — where he comes from—how he moves—where he goes to.

If they choose to they can make it a poem in three sections, as Roger McGough did with *Bully Night*.

★ If it has not already arisen ask the class how they feel about the last verse. Why does the poem end so abruptly? If they know *Not Me* (see Section 10) it may influence their judgement.

★ Make copies of the poem available for children to work on a reading. A group of three might each select and prepare one of the verses; readings may be presented to the full class or another class. If possible have a cassette player available for any groups who choose to record their reading.

★ If it seems appropriate, talk about fears in general. What other things frighten people? Dogs? Heights? What might adults be afraid of?

RELATED POEMS

Shrieks at midnight—Dorothy Brown Thompson—and *Fear* and *Running home*—Barbara Ireson—in 'Rhyme Time 2'—comp. Barbara Ireson—Beaver Books.

Noises in the Night—William McCrea—*Night Shapes*—Paddy Kinsale—and *In the Dark*—Jane Pridmore—in 'Poetry Plus: Green Earth and Silver Stars'—comp. B. R. Marney *et al.*—Schofield and Sims.

I like to stay up—Grace Nichols—in 'I Like That Stuff'—comp. Morag Styles—Cambridge University Press.

What's That?—Florence Parry Heide—in 'Monster Poems'—ed. Daisy Wallace—Piccadilly Press.

Fever Dream—Edward Lowbury—in 'All Sorts of Poems'—ed. Ann Thwaite—Magnet.

Peeling and feeling

SECTION 8

Imagine being inside a balloon. Feel and push against the side.

Poems sometimes illuminate each other, in the sense that one sets up a train of thought or feeling which the next one extends. This is often a personal connection: as you read a poem some element within it recalls just a line, a phrase or a word in a poem you already know and like.

The connection in the following pair of poems is obvious. The balloon/balloonman idea, the colour, the movement, the sound patterns and the sense of child/children are common elements. The second is as complex as the first is simple, but that in itself recommended *The Balloon* as a way into *in Just-spring*.

It is an interesting reflection on the capacity of young children for response to complex material when it fires their imaginations that the cummings' poem has been requested frequently since, but *The Balloon*— apparently enjoyed when it was first introduced and which led to some fine pictures for the classroom wall and to sensitive movement—has never been called for again.

The Balloon

I went to the park

And I bought a balloon.

It sailed through the sky

Like a large orange moon.

It bumped and it fluttered

And swam with the clouds.

Small birds flew around it

In high chirping crowds.

It bounced and it balanced

And bowed with the breeze.

It skimmed past the leaves

On the tops of the trees.

And then as the day

Started turning to night

I gave a short jump

And I held the string tight

And home we all sailed

Through the darkening sky,

The orange balloon, the small birds

And I.

Karla Kuskin

in Just-spring

In Just-
spring   when the world is mud-
luscious the little
lame balloonman

whistles   far   and wee

and eddieandbill come
running from marbles and
piracies and it's
spring

when the world is puddle-wonderful

the queer
old balloonman whistles
far   and   wee
and bettyandisbel come dancing

from hop-scotch and jump-rope and

it's
spring
and

     the

       goat-footed

balloonMan   whistles
far
and
wee

e.e. cummings

FIRST ENCOUNTERS

★ (i) Position the children in a circle and pass around a variety of balloons. Encourage them to use as many as possible of their senses to explore their properties. Ask them to speak out loud any words which might describe them, such as *light, rubbery, red, transparent.*

(ii) Free play with a varied collection of balloons can lead naturally into movement work without balloons:

(a) Imagine tapping a balloon up and down on the palm of your hand.

(b) Imagine walking with a balloon on a string, being careful not to tangle your string with anyone else's.

(c) Select a balloon shape to grow into—possibly with a suitable sound effect for this movement—then, at a signal, burst into another shape.

(d) Imagine being inside a balloon. Feel and push against the side. Call out words that describe how you feel.

(iii) Conclude the session by settling the group around you and reading the two poems with the declared intention of looking at them again later.

★ (i) Read both the poems twice. If possible use another reader so that each poem is spoken by two different voices. Alternatively, if this is more convenient, you might tape readings by another voice.

(ii) Talk about their first impressions. Why do they think you have chosen to link the poems together? What similarities or differences do they notice between them?

DEVELOPMENTS

★ (i) Ask the children to build a visual picture in their heads while you read or play a tape recording of *The Balloon*. If they are unsure about this you might prompt with some questions:

— what shape is the balloon?

— where is it flying?

— what is underneath?

— what does the person holding it look like?

56

(ii) Encourage the children to share the pictures they formed. If you listened along with them you can also talk about your picture.

(iii) Provide a choice of materials for individual paintings or collages of the poem.

★ (i) Re-read *in Just-spring*, then ask the children to imagine they have seen the balloonman of the poem.

(ii) With the children in role as those who have just seen the balloonman and you in role as someone who knows nothing of him, encourage the children to explore the character within the poem whilst supplying you with information.

(iii) Provide charcoal and pastel crayons for individual portraits of how the balloonman might look.

★ (i) Using either books or an overhead projector show the children how the two poems look on the page (a useful thing to do with any poem). The contrast between the regularity of *The Balloon* and the irregular divisions, spaces, line lengths and overall visual impression of *in Just-spring* may well provoke spontaneous comment. If not, encourage them to look for differences and to say what they think accounts for them.

(ii) Refer back to the words which arose in the first of the suggested introductions of this section (if you did it) or ask afresh for words associated with the touch, smell, sight and movement, of balloons. When you have accumulated enough, combine them to make a class balloon poem. In addition or as an alternative encourage individuals to produce their own poems set against the background of a balloon shape. In this way a whole 'cluster' of poems may provide a wall display or a lasting class book.

EXTRA

★ Individuals may enjoy writing a story about what they imagine happens to the child in *The Balloon* between floating into the sky and arriving home, or the story that one of the children in *in Just-spring* tells afterwards either at home or at school about the balloonman in the park.

RELATED POEMS

Balloons—Judith Thurman—*Scarecrow Independence*—James Kirkup—*Flying*—
J. M. Westrup—and *Windy Nights*—R. L. Stevenson—in 'A First Poetry
Book'—comp. John Foster—Oxford University Press.

Balloons . . . Balloons—Myra Cohn Livingstone—in 'When a Goose Meets a
Moose'—comp. C. Scott Mitchell—Evans Bros.

Someone—Walter de la Mare—in 'Secret Laughter'—Puffin.

One Misty Moisty Morning—Traditional—in 'The Puffin Book of Nursery
Rhymes'—comp. Iona and Peter Opie—Puffin.

The Intruder—James Reeves—in 'A Puffin Quarter of Poets'—comp. Eleanor
Graham—Puffin.

summer
is
flowery
bowery
Winter
nippy
freezy
wheezy
Sneezy
Autumn
showery
croppy
drippy
slippy
spring
poppy
hoppy.

Be prepared for groups
to value their own
version more highly
than the original.

Turning the pages of a poetry book you are sometimes struck by the possibilities that a poem suggests to you. You are fired as much by enthusiasm for what it might lead to as by the poem itself.

This section centres on a very simple poem. Each line begins with one of the four seasons. Associated with each season there are three words that differ only in their initial consonants. The overall impact is striking and pleasing. There is an underlying humour.

Immediately it suggests other possible patterns using the same words. It also suggests an opportunity to observe how a group goes about shaping a poem and making sense of words that are only partly familiar.

```
┌─────────────────────────────────────────┐
│              SPRING IS                   │
│  Spring is showery, flowery, bowery;     │
│  Summer  :  hoppy, croppy, poppy;        │
│  Autumn  :  wheezy, sneezy, freezy;      │
│  Winter  :  slippy, drippy, nippy.       │
│                              Anon.        │
└─────────────────────────────────────────┘
```

Alternative versions produced by groups of 6–7 year olds given 'packs' of cards, each with a word from 'Spring is', and asked to make a poem from them:

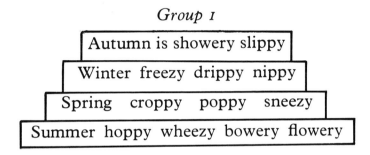

Group 1

| Autumn is showery slippy |
| Winter freezy drippy nippy |
| Spring croppy poppy sneezy |
| Summer hoppy wheezy bowery flowery |

Group 2

```
Summer
is
flowery
bowery
Winter
nippy
freezy
wheezy
sneezy
Autumn
showery
croppy
drippy
slippy
Spring
poppy
happy
```

FIRST ENCOUNTER

★ (i) Prepare separate cards on which are written the individual words that make up the poem. These should be large enough to be handled and read by a group of four or five children who might choose to work on the floor.

(ii) Present a pack of word cards to groups of no more than five children. Read through the cards until all the words can be recognised. Explain that these are the words of a poem which you have jumbled up.

(iii) Explain the task to the group: they are to work co-operatively to produce their own poem using the given words in any order or sequence they feel 'works' for them. Make sure they understand that there is not a right or wrong solution; the aim is simply to produce a poem that pleases them. Take time to make clear that majority decisions are to be aimed at and encourage them to 'test' the sound of their poem by reading and re-reading it as it takes shape. (If it is possible to observe groups while they work, without inhibiting them, see how the members of the group relate to one another and organise themselves on a task without anyone in authority. Note also the ways in which the children 'sort' the words by logic, intuition, sound patterns, or a combination of a variety of strategies.)

(iv) Make a copy of the poem or poems produced within each group for reading aloud later.

(v) Discuss the activity with them:

— how did you begin sorting the words?

— why did you choose that pattern?

— did you disagree about any part of it—if so, why?

— how did you decide whose ideas to use?

— what would you call the poem?

★ (i) Each group prepares a reading of their poem and shares it with the others. There is added interest in comparing the visual pattern of each on paper— done most quickly and efficiently with acetate sheets on an overhead projector.

(ii) Read the original poem and present its written pattern for everyone to see. (This will be their first encounter with the poem in its original form.)

(iii) Discuss all the poems. Be prepared for groups to value their own versions more highly than the original.

EXTRA

★ Using the names of the four seasons in order, suggest that children supply three or four descriptive words to accompany each season to produce a poem of their own. They might work individually, in pairs, or in small groups with you assisting by suggesting words and acting as scribe.

(It is obvious that not all children will have experienced the seasons in quite the same way as depicted in this poem. Having a class of children from widely varied backgrounds may result in some interesting discussion and sharply contrasting poems. It need not prevent this particular poem being used as a model.)

RELATED POEMS, suitable as models

The Prayer of the Little Ducks Who Went into the Ark—Carman Bernos de Gasztold—in 'Junior Voices Book 1'—ed. Geoffrey Summerfield—Penguin.

My Cat Likes to Hide in Boxes—Eve Sutton—Picture Puffin.

Hairy Maclary from Donaldson's Dairy—Lynley Dodd—Picture Puffin.

Slowly—James Reeves—in 'Wordscapes'—comp. Barry Maybury—Oxford University Press.

SECTION 10

Include sessions where individual choices are welcomed and comments on personal likes and dislikes can be voiced.

SECOND HELPINGS

All of the poems in this section are second helpings: poems that we have read to the class on previous occasions. Some were initially chosen by us, some were chosen by us to read by children browsing through the stack of poetry books in the classroom, but in each case they made sufficient impression to be chosen on one particular afternoon when we sat in a circle and children requested favourites. The sample given is their genuine selection.

One of the choices is particularly interesting, showing how mysteriously chance plays a part in our successes. *Cows* by James Reeves received a disappointingly muted response when first read to the class. Soon afterwards we made one of our frequent tapes of five poems for the class to play at leisure, and we included it. The recording played back had a distant but clear cow's moo at the end of the poem. Neither of us was aware of the sound when we recorded and can offer no explanation. There are no cows now within sight or sound of the school, though a farm did once stand here. This added intrigue to the normal interest the class showed in the recordings we made for them. This poem on the tape has now been replayed so regularly that most of the class can repeat it from memory and, as demonstrated by this selection, it has become a favourite.

The response to an invitation to choose favourites may be an indication of how far you are arousing real pleasure through poems. If you have to work hard to get any requests it may be that the connection between poetry and delight is still to be made.

Why?

I'm just going out for a moment.

Why?

To make a cup of tea.

Why?

Because I'm thirsty.

Why?

Because it's hot.

Why?

Because the sun's shining.

Why?

Because it's summer.

Why?

Because that's when it is.

Why?

Why don't you stop saying why?

Why?

Tea-time why.
High-time-you-stopped-
                saying-why-time.

What?

Michael Rosen

Please Mrs Butler

Please Mrs Butler
This boy Derek Drew
Keeps copying my work, Miss.
What shall I do?

Go and sit in the hall, dear.
Go and sit in the sink.
Take your books on the roof, my lamb.
Do whatever you think.

Please Mrs Butler
This boy Derek Drew
Keeps taking my rubber, Miss.
What shall I do?

Keep it in your hand, dear.
Hide it up your vest.
Swallow it if you like, my love.
Do what you think best.

Please Mrs Butler
This boy Derek Drew
Keeps calling me rude names, Miss.
What shall I do?

Lock yourself in the cupboard, dear.
Run away to sea.
Do whatever you can, my flower.
But don't ask me!

Allan Ahlberg

Cows

Half the time they munched the grass, and all the time they lay
Down in the water-meadows, the lazy month of May,
    A-chewing,
    A-mooing,
  To pass the hours away.
  "Nice weather," said the brown cow.
    "Ah," said the white.
  "Grass is very tasty."
    "Grass is all right."

Half the time they munched the grass, and all the time they lay
Down in the water-meadows, the lazy month of May,
    A-chewing,
    A-mooing,
  To pass the hours away.
  "Rain coming," said the brown cow.
    "Ah," said the white.
  "Flies is very tiresome."
    "Flies bite."

Half the time they munched the grass, and all the time they lay
Down in the water-meadows, the lazy month of May,
    A-chewing,
    A-mooing,
  To pass the hours away.
  "Time to go," said the brown cow.
    "Ah," said the white.
  "Nice chat." "Very pleasant."
    "Night." "Night."

Half the time they munched the grass, and all the time they lay
Down in the water-meadows, the lazy month of May,
    A-chewing,
    A-mooing,
  To pass the hours away.

James Reeves

Not Me

The Slithergadee has crawled out of the sea.
He may catch all the others, but he
        won't catch me.
No you won't catch me, old slithergadee,
You may catch all the others, but you wo—

Shel Silverstein

The Hairy Toe

Once there was a woman went out to pick beans,
and she found a Hairy Toe.
She took the Hairy Toe home with her,
and that night, when she went to bed,
the wind began to moan and groan.
Away off in the distance
she seemed to hear a voice crying,
'Who's got my Hair-r-ry To-o-oe?
Who's got my Hair-r-ry To-o-oe?'

The woman scrooched down,
'way down under the covers,
and about that time
the wind appeared to hit the house,
smoosh,
and the old house creaked and cracked
like something was trying to get in.
The voice had come nearer,
almost at the door now,
and it said,
'Where's my Hair-r-ry To-o-oe?
Who's got my Hair-r-ry To-o-oe?'

The woman scrooched further down
under the covers
and pulled them tight around her head.
The wind growled around the house
like some big animal
and r-r-um-mbled
over the chimbley.
All at once she heard the door cr-r-a-ack
and Something slipped in
and began to creep over the floor.
The floor went
cre-e-eak, cre-e-eak
at every step that thing took towards her bed.
The woman could almost feel
it bending over her bed.
Then in an awful voice it said:
'Where's my Hair-r-ry To-o-oe?
Who's got my Hair-r-ry To-o-oe?
You've got it!'   *Traditional American*

70

SOME WAYS OF ENJOYING 'SECOND HELPINGS'

Record or tape a selection of poems chosen by the class.
Use other voices to add variation but make sure these are familiar to the children.
(Our experience is that known voices appeal most to young children, so commercial tapes may not be a good buy.)

Tape selections with your class present. They may enjoy the sense of occasion at these times and may be able to join in at appropriate points. Small background noises need not be intrusive, and will make the tapes more the children's own.

Prepare tapes to exchange with another class or school.
If the children are unable to read the poems themselves they could join in with certain appropriate lines or choruses.

When children have established a collection of favourites help them to organise 'let's hear them again' sessions.

Make a group of children from the class responsible for the choice of poems to be included in a session. They might also work on a presentation of some or all of their choices. (Groups can obviously change in order to give the whole class the opportunity of selecting poems for future sessions.)

Invite another class to join a live poetry 'swap'. This could lead to a wall display, in both classrooms, of a copy of each of the poems read.

Encourage visitors (providing they understand the needs of your group) to share some poems and at the same time provide a new audience for the children's own choice of poems.

★ With the help of the class, select one or two poems for groups of children to prepare different presentations.
Share all the presentations at one session and talk about the differences.

★ Pick a theme for a session, such as animals, weather, feelings, or nonsense. Divide the class into groups and let each group select one or more poems on the chosen subject, which can later be shared by all.

★ Include sessions where individuals' choices are welcomed and comments on personal likes and dislikes can be voiced.

PART TWO

Approaches to some of the activities referred to in Part One.

1. BROWSING AND SHARING

We found that children enjoyed sitting and reading from a poetry book together, often with one child reading and the other listening. Sometimes four or five children squashed up together on one big chair.

It is a good idea to provide time when small groups can browse amongst an interesting collection of poetry books (see Part III) or sit and listen to poetry cassettes which you have made with them or for them, or which they have made themselves.

You can also encourage browsing by setting aside times for children to bring you poems they have found for you to read and share with them. This can lead to surprising demonstrations of initiative and judgement. A six year old reacted to first hearing Eve Sutton's *My Cat Likes to Hide in Boxes* with the comment 'That's like *Hairy Maclary from Donaldson's Dairy*' (both Picture Puffins). Because this was one of the books ready to hand he was able immediately to demonstrate what he meant. On several occasions, after hearing a poem they enjoyed, children spent browsing time finding other poems by the same writer or on a related topic. They spent as much time looking for poems that we would enjoy as we spent finding poems for them.

2. CHOOSING POEMS FOR A CLASS

Choice by the teacher should really come from browsing amongst a variety of poetry books: what's good for the pupil is good for the teacher. The ideal time— for excellent educational reasons—is when the pupils too are browsing (another possible application of time devoted to USSR—Uninterrupted, Sustained, Silent Reading—when *everyone* in the school is seen to be taking part).

There are many reasons for choosing a particular poem. We might sum them up as:

— you like it and want to read it to the class.

— you think the class will like it. (This may be a rational or an instinctive judgement.)

— it has some particular quality you want to introduce to the class or which you feel they might enjoy, be stirred by, or otherwise respond to.

— it suggests to you a connection with some other activity and you want to pursue the connection.

74

If you still have problems in making choices some guiding principles might be:

— trust your own judgement.

— don't underestimate the children: they will sometimes astonish you by responding enthusiastically to a poem you find challenging. Not all the words in a poem have to be familiar.

—aim in the long term for a wide variety, including much that you consider slight but entertaining.

An important supplementary principle:

— provide frequent occasions when the pupils themselves choose the poem.

3. CLASS OR GROUP DISCUSSION OF A POEM

The best questions for arousing discussion leave room for more than one answer and invite different viewpoints. Remember that your concern is to come closer to the poem, rather than encouraging children to 'bounce away' from the poem through random trains of thought it may have set in motion. Initially, ask questions that you know some of the class, at least, will be able to answer, which will help *all* children to engage with the poem. Use your own questions as starters to throw in when contributions from the children dry up.

Questions that might stimulate discussion:

(i) *Factual*

How many characters are talking in the poem? Why are they quarrelling? (*Overheard on a Saltmarsh*)

How many animals come into the poem? Who are the people that the poem tells us about? (*Mister Fox*)

Where do the events of the poem happen? (Almost any poem)

(ii) *Speculative/Interpretative*

Why do you think the goblin wants the beads? (*Overheard on a Saltmarsh*)

How did Mrs. Slipper-Slopper happen to wake up when the fox went off with the grey goose? (*Mister Fox*)

What do you think might have happened afterwards? (Almost any poem)

Do you think the nymph should have given the beads to the goblin? (*Overheard on a Saltmarsh*)

What do you think of the fox? (*Mister Fox*)

What pictures did you see in your head as you heard the poem? (Almost any poem)

Were there any words or groups of words that you specially liked? (Almost any poem)

As with all other activities suggested, don't labour a discussion once the group is clearly losing interest. But do find your own techniques for nudging the discussion along if that is all that is needed.

4. DRAWING AND PAINTING

Some children choose to illustrate a part of a poem or a feeling it conveys without any prompting. A variety of materials should always be available.

Sometimes you may suggest exploring, through drawing, a particular aspect of a poem. In this case encourage the children to consider the suitability of materials they select and to explain why they have made their choices.

Be prepared to advise but also encourage the children to seek the views of others in the class. This should sometimes lead naturally to collaborative work involving discussion—including argument—focussed on the poem being illustrated (see Part I, Section 3). Whichever way you choose to work it is important to allow time for children to produce a piece of work with which they feel reasonably satisfied. Resist any temptation to fill in a final five minutes after a poetry reading with 'drawing a picture' unless you consider the drawings to be preliminary sketches or an important means of holding first reactions.

Once the paintings/drawings are complete there remain the numerous choices of what to do with them. You might:

(i) Let the child take the work home. Some children genuinely feel a need to share their work with their own family. They may later return the work for display.

(ii) Use the completed picture(s) as a basis for group discussion. Questions can be raised both by you and the class:

— do you think the colours tell us anything about the poem?

— would the painting/drawing have been better on a different background?

— why have you drawn 'X' with that expression on his face?

76

(iii) Mount the paintings/drawings appropriately. Some children may do this for themselves, others may need a little help. Display the mounted work alongside the poem or the lines of the poem it relates to. This may give rise to more discussion.

(iv) Use them as a basis for a class book.

Once art work is removed from display, or ceases to be a teaching point, return it to the artist or keep it to show at 'let's hear them again' sessions. (See *Second Helpings*)

5. RHYTHM AND SOUND

Playing with rhythm and sound is a necessary part of language development. Encourage this sort of play by exploring the rhythms and sounds of the children's own names and words they commonly use. Can they invent words to represent any of the sounds that surround them daily, as Clive Sansom did with 'jicketty-can' to suggest the sound of a train? What about a vacuum cleaner? A motor-bike?

Combine words to make aural and visual patterns—both are common in poetry as is demonstrated by *in Just-spring*, *Bully Night* and *Alone in the Grange*. Set aside a corner with a cassette player where the children can play with sound and rhythm in relation to words. Include recordings which you have made for them—possibly with them. Encourage them to experiment. Have on display copies of poems which make particular play with rhythm and sound such as *The Train* and those listed in that section's 'Related Poems'.

Now and then draw attention to the way rhythm, rhyme and other sound patterns are working in a poem and ask for comments on the effect they achieve. There is probably no point in labelling in a formal way—it is sufficient, for example, to note that 'sweet' and 'fleet' echo the same sound.

Occasionally you might look at a contrast, such as Peter Young's use of rhythm and sound in *Hands* and Roger McGough's in the last verse of *Bully Night*. The questions to be asked may be: *what are the writers trying to do?* and *how are they doing it?*

6. MOVEMENT

Any movement used to explore a poem in depth needs space, time and commitment from both teacher and child. You may be:

(i) Exploring actions or movements described in a poem:

. . . taking and breaking . . . (*Hands*)

(ii) Exploring movements appropriate to characters within a poem:

> . . . Soft,
> Soft,
> Are his steps as he climbs . . . (*Alone in the Grange*)

(iii) Using movement to suggest abstract qualities and moods in the poem:

> . . . And where's the dog,
> And must it drown? . . . (*The Rescue*)

(iv) Combining a series of movements to interpret a complete poem. Work on whole body movements should be balanced with finer movements involving parts of the body. The latter make greater demands in terms of effort and concentration. Encourage children to describe their movements verbally.

Try to ensure that children have opportunities to work individually and co-operatively: in pairs, groups of three to six and as a class.

Make sure that they are observed and that they observe others at work. Encourage them to praise and offer constructive criticism at these times. You can always redress the balance if you consider comments too harsh.

Don't rush from one piece of movement to another too rapidly. Children need time to rehearse and perfect their movements, especially when working with others. Be aware of individuals' capabilities and aim to stretch and encourage accordingly.

7. DRAMA

There are basic drama activities which any interested teacher can manage quite readily. All of the following are valuable for exploring poetry.

(i) *Improvisation:* bringing alive through characterisation, interaction, movement. Appropriate subjects are the conflicts within the poem (such as the impact in a farmyard when a fox appears), or the context in which the poem is set (such as a beach when a storm is brewing). Judge the success of the improvisation by the conviction and imagination with which the children create the scene and their own part in it. Let them comment on and evaluate the work of other groups.

(ii) *Still photographs:* pairs or small groups work on a frozen moment from the poem, which they create as a photographer would compose his picture. (One member of the group may well take charge as the photographer.) The aim is for a two-dimensional effect and they should be viewed accordingly.

(iii) *Tableaux/Sculptures:* a different form of frozen moment—the work of a sculptor rather than a photographer. Again, one member of the group may take on that role. The visual impression should be considered from all angles and the viewers invited to walk around.

(iv) *Freezing*: a technique for stopping dramatic action at a signal from the person in control. Very useful for deepening concentration and examining critically details of the drama or improvisation at a particular moment—facial expression, posture, movement, and so on.

(v) *Slow Motion:* a technique for focussing attention, particularly useful when the dramatic work is sloppy or thoughtless. A means of exploring such things as how movements develop and how the body externally reflects inner experience.

8. ROLE-PLAY

If the class have never worked 'in role' you have to explain carefully what will happen before attempting any role-play. Use the words 'going into role' so that this becomes a familiar phrase but qualify this by setting the scene and situation very clearly. For example:

> *Close your eyes. When I tell you to open them I won't be Mrs. Balaam I shall be Noah. You are my family and have helped me build the Ark. Some of the people in the town have been complaining because we are saving ourselves and leaving them to drown. We have to decide what we are going to do about it.*

When this technique is first used it may be easier for the class to talk to the person in role whilst they stay themselves. When they do go into role spend time making sure everyone understands the rules of the activity and give the children some time to think about the characters they will be role-playing.

Each teacher will evolve her own ways of doing this. One way might be to ask the children to close their eyes and think about their new roles. Pose some questions that the children can silently think about:

— how old are you?

— where do you live?

— what are you wearing?

— are you kind/angry/miserable/frightened?

Obviously these questions will vary according to the roles to be adopted.

79

Once the children understand something of what is entailed in 'going into role' you may wish to devise a signal in order to indicate the beginning and end of role play:

When I click my fingers the role play will begin. When I repeat the signal we will all be ourselves again.

If you feel anxious about the level of the group's commitment you might also negotiate a signal which will halt the role play should belief in what is happening collapse.

It is not necessary to alter your voice in role, unless the character really demands it. Remember to vary the roles you or the children adopt. You may prefer a role of authority in order to maintain control but much can be gained from assuming the role of someone in need of help and/or information and allowing children to assume a helpful, knowledgeable role.

Role play need not last for any set time. Five minutes may provide some very interesting results whilst other sessions may last 20–30 minutes without signs of flagging. Whatever the length of the session, there needs to be time for discussion when ideas and opinions stemming from role-work can be voiced.

9. PRESENTATION

The preparation of a poem for presentation to other people is not only an enjoyable classroom activity, but also a way into appreciation of that poem for both the presenters and the listeners.

Once established as a classroom activity it needs little prompting and the variations from simple to complex seem endless.

A child who has found a poem and wants to read it to the teacher is offering the simplest form of presentation. At the other extreme is the full class presentation of a programme of varied poems which all have helped to select, prepare and taken part in. This might include a combination of drama, movement, mime, art, music and so on. The audience in this case may be another class, the whole school, or even another school with which an exchange of poetry entertainment has been arranged.

Some variables should be encouraged as a matter of policy. Everyone at some time perhaps might experience the responsibility of preparing a solo or group presentation for a small audience. If some find it easier when the audience is invisible, a cassette recording may serve. Similarly everyone at some time might experience taking part in a presentation which associates a poem with the kinds of activities we have described in other sections. It is possible to vary the extent and the nature of the involvement to allow for the shyest children, as demonstrated by one of our boys who sat behind a piano with an alert triangle (*The Shark*: Lalla Ward).

Another important variable is choosing the poem. There are positive gains in expecting pupils to find poems which they would like to work on for presentation. It is an occasion for browsing and making choices. If they are in groups it is an occasion for purposeful discussion. But there are also occasions when there is real value in working on a poem selected by someone else. It is exciting, for example, for a group to be given a poem with a set time allowed for preparing a presentation, knowing that each of the other groups has been given a different poem and that all will come together in a miniature poetry show when the time runs out.

PART THREE

BOOK-LISTS

One way of generating enthusiasm for poems is to have a large number and a wide range of attractive poetry books around. In school a collection of 30–40 books in a box or a case is portable and can be used by several classes. It leads naturally to activities like browsing, choosing, rejecting, selecting for personal anthologies, sharing personal choices, and articulating reasons for likes and dislikes.

The following lists are guides to some of the poetry books suitable for children in the early years which are available. We have suggested collections of 30–40 books in the hope that schools may have funds to put together at least one portable poetry box. Each collection contains titles which include poems from a range of cultures.

† signifies paperback
★ signifies a choice between an edition with words and music, or with words only

A COLLECTION OF POETRY BOOKS FOR THE EARLY YEARS I

1.	I Din Do Nuttin and Other Poems †	John Agard	Magnet
2.	Say It Again, Granny!	John Agard	Bodley Head
3.	Hob and Other Poems	Michael Baldwin	Chatto and Windus
4.	The Alphabetical Zoo	George Barker	Faber
5.	Selected Cautionary Verses †	Hilaire Belloc	Puffin
6.	Roger was a Razor fish †	Jill Bennett	Bodley Head
7.	Oxford Book of Poetry for Children †	Edward Blishen	Oxford
8.	And I Dance	Keith Bosley	Angus and Robertson
9.	The Mother Goose Treasury †	Raymond Briggs	Picture Puffin
10.	The Hunting of the Snark	Lewis Carroll	Chatto and Windus
11.	Jabberwocky and Other Poems	Lewis Carroll	Faber
12.	Figure of 8	Charles Causley	Macmillan
13.	Figgie Hobbin †	Charles Causley	Puffin
14.	The Puffin Book of Magic Verse †	Charles Causley	Puffin
15.	Stir-about	Nancy Chambers	Julia MacRae
16.	Hi-Ran-Ho!	Aidan and Nancy Chambers	Longman
17.	The Wood is Sweet	John Clare	Bodley Head
18.	The Singing Time	Leonard Clark	Hodder and Stoughton
19.	Secret as Toads	Leonard Clark	Chatto and Windus
20.	Oh, Such Foolishness †	William Cole	Magnet
21.	Come Hither †	Walter de la Mare	Puffin
22.	The Word Party	Richard Edwards	Lutterworth Press
23.	Silver-Sand and Snow	Eleanor Farjeon	Michael Joseph
24.	Funny Folk	Robert Fisher	Faber
25.	You Come Too	Robert Frost	Bodley Head
26.	A Book of Seasons	Eve Garnett	Oxford
27.	Under the Window	Kate Greenaway	Warne and Co.
28.	One, Two, Three, Four	Mary Grice	Warne and Co
29.	A House is a House for Me †	Mary Ann Hoberman	Picture Puffin
30.	Moon-bells and Other Poems	Ted Hughes	Chatto and Windus
31.	The Young Puffin Book of Verse †	Barbara Ireson	Puffin
32.	Just Around the Corner	L. B. Jacobs	Evans Bros.
33.	Ducks and Dragons †	Gene Kemp	Faber

34.	Whiskers and Rhymes	Arnold Lobel	Julia MacRae
35.	Poems for Seven Year olds and Under †	Helen Nicoll	Puffin
36.	You Can't Catch Me†	Michael Rosen	Picture Puffin
37.	My Cat Likes to Hide in Boxes †	Eve Sutton	Picture Puffin

A COLLECTION OF POETRY BOOKS FOR THE EARLY YEARS II

1.	Please Mrs. Butler †	Allan Ahlberg	Puffin
2.	Tinder Box †	Sylvia Barratt and Sheena Hodge	Black
3.	A Packet of Poems	Jill Bennett	Oxford
4.	Quentin Blake's Nursery Rhyme Book †	Quentin Blake	Picture Lions
5.	Nonsense Rhymes †	Peggy Blakely	Black
6.	The Parrot in the Garret	Leonore Blegvad	Julia MacRae
7.	Mango Spice: 44 Carribean Songs †	Gloria Cameron *et. al.*	Black
8.	Merrily to Bethlehem †★	Cameron *et al.*	Black
9.	Harlequin †★	Cameron *et al.*	Black
10.	Alleluja! †★	Cameron *et al.*	Black
11.	All Along Down Along	Leonard Clark	Longman
12.	Peacock Pie †	Walter de la Mare	Fanfare
13.	Hairy Maclary from Donaldson's Dairy †	Lynley Dodd	Picture Puffin
14.	The Wind Has Wings	Mary Alice Downie and Barbara Robertson	Oxford
15.	A Very First Poetry Book †	John Foster	Oxford
16.	A First Poetry Book †	John Foster	Oxford
17.	Rhyme Time Book 1 †	Barbara Ireson	Beaver
18.	Rhyme Time Book 2 †	Barbara Ireson	Beaver
19.	Old Merlaine	Cara Lockhart-Smith	Heinemann
20.	Mr. Bidery's Spidery Garden	David McCord	Harrap
21.	This Little Puffin †	Elizabeth Matterson	Puffin
22.	Silly Verse for Kids †	Spike Milligan	Puffin
23.	When We Were Very Young †	A. A. Milne	Methuen
24.	Now We Are Six †	A. A. Milne	Methuen
25.	The Puffin Book of Nursery Rhymes †	Peter and Iona Opie	Puffin

26. The Wandering Moon	James Reeves	Heinemann
27. A Book of Nonsense	Ernest Rhys	Dent
28. You Tell Me †	Michael Rosen and Roger McGough	Puffin
29. The Kingfisher Book of Children's Poetry	Michael Rosen	Kingfisher
30. Goblin Market †	Christina Rossetti	Harrap
31. Mother Goose Comes to Cable Street†	Rosemary Stones and Andrew Mann	Picture Puffin
32. Rain Falling Sun Shining†	Odette Thomas	Bogle l'Ouverture
33. Hot Dog and Other Poems†	Kit Wright	Puffin

A COLLECTION OF POETRY BOOKS FOR THE EARLY YEARS III

1. Tiny Tim: Verses for Children†	Jill Bennett	Picture Lions
2. The Great Big Book of Nursery Rhymes	Peggy Blakely	Black
3. Once Upon a Rhyme†	Sara and Stephen Corrin	Puffin
4. The Book of Verse for Children	R. L. Green	Dent
5. The Faber Book of Nursery Verse†	Barbara Ireson	Faber
6. The Troublesome Pig†	Priscilla Lamont	Piccolo
7. A Calendar of Poems	Wes Magee	Bell and Hyman
8. Muslim Nursery Rhymes†	Mustapha McDermott	The Islamic Foundation
9. Here a Little Child I Stand	Cynthia Mitchell	Heinemann
10. Playtime	Cynthia Mitchell	Heinemann
11. Old Fashioned Nursery Rhymes†	Jennifer Mulherin	Granada
12. The Oxford Nursery Rhyme Book	Iona and Peter Opie	Oxford
13. Song of the City†	Gareth Owen	Fontana
14. Round About Eight	Geoffrey Palmer and Noel Lloyd	Warne
15. Beatrix Potter's Nursery Rhyme Book†	Beatrix Potter	Viking Kestrel
16. The Mother Goose Book†	A. and M. Provensen	Beaver
17. Inky Pinky Ponky: Children's Playground Rhymes†	Michael Rosen and Susannah Steele	Granada
18. Speech Rhymes	Clive Sansom	Black

19.	Creatures Small†	Saunders and Williams	Evans
20.	Weathers and Seasons†	Saunders and Williams	Evans
21.	Colours†	Saunders and Williams	Evans
22.	Thomas and the Sparrow	Ian Serraillier	Oxford
23.	The Robin and the Wren	Ian Serraillier	Oxford
24.	Happily Ever After	Ian Serraillier	Oxford
25.	A Light in the Attic	Shel Silverstein	Cape
26.	My Kind of Verse	John Smith	Burke
27.	Blue Bell Hill Games†	R. A. Smith	Young Puffin
28.	The Green Roads	Edward Thomas	Bodley Head
29.	Children as Poets†	Denys Thompson	Heinemann
30.	Flashlight and Other Poems†	Judith Thurman	Kestrel
31.	Fun and Nonsense	Louis Untermeyer	Western Publishing Company
32.	Dragon Night and Other Lullabies	Jane Yolen	Methuen

POETRY BOOKS REFERRED TO UNDER 'RELATED POEMS'

Days Are Where We Live	Bennett	Bodley Head
The Oxford Book of Children's Verse†	Blishen	Oxford
Through the Looking Glass†	Carroll	Various
Figgie Hobbin†	Causley	Puffin
The Puffin Book of Magic Verse†	Causley	Puffin
Secret Laughter†	de la Mare	Puffin
Invitation to a Mouse†	Farjeon	Knight
A Puffin Quartet of Poets†	Farjeon, Reeves, Rieu, Serraillier	Puffin
A Very First Poetry Book†	Foster	Oxford
A First Poetry Book†	Foster	Oxford
Rhyme Time, Books 1 and 2†	Ireson	Beaver
Poems and Pictures: Night†	McKellar and Baldwin	Evans
Poems and Pictures: Ourselves	McKellar and Baldwin	Evans
Poetry Plus: Green Earth and Silver Stars†	Marney	Schofield and Sims

This Little Puffin†	Matterson	Puffin
Wordscapes†	Maybury	Oxford
Old Fashioned Nursery Rhymes†	Mulherin	Granada
Poems for Seven Year Olds and Under†	Nicoll	Puffin
The Puffin Book of Nursery Rhymes†	Opie and Opie	Puffin
You Can't Catch Me†	Rosen and Blake	Picture Puffin
Sing-Song: A Nursery Rhyme Book (1872)†	Rossetti	Dover
When a Goose Meets a Moose	Scott-Mitchell	Evans
A Child's Garden of Verses†	Stevenson	Puffin
I Like That Stuff†	Styles	Cambridge
Junior Voices Book 1†	Summerfield	Penguin
Welcome and Other Poems	Summerfield	Deutsch
My Cat Likes to Hide in Boxes†	Sutton	Picture Puffin
All Sorts of Poems†	Thwaite	Magnet
Monster Poems	Wallace	Piccadilly

THE SIX MOST HANDLED BOOKS IN THE CLASSES WE WORKED WITH

Please Mrs Butler†	Ahlberg	Puffin
Tiny Tim†	Bennett	Armada
A First Poetry Book†	Foster	Oxford
You Tell Me†	McGough and Rosen	Puffin
Poems for Seven Year Olds and Under†	Nicoll	Puffin
A Light in the Attic	Silverstein	Cape

OTHER NATE PUBLICATIONS
by Brian Merrick

EXPLORING POETRY: 8–13

Teaching poetry may present a variety of problems. How *do* you devise a successful poetry teaching programme? What part might the class itself play in shaping such a programme? What poetry is appropriate for the age group, and for individual pupils, and where can it be found?

The wealth of material published in recent years has provided teachers and pupils alike with rich resources to draw on, but this in turn gives rise to problems of choice. Then there is the need to devise activities that help children to explore the poems successfully, to make them their own.

Brian Merrick draws on his own experience and that of other teachers and student-teachers in the South West of England in offering some answers to these questions. This book carries forward and further develops the ideas put forward in the highly successful *Exploring Poetry: 5-8*.

In **Exploring Poetry: 8-13** Brian Merrick begins by considering some principles and some well-tried practices. This general survey is followed by a detailed sequence of work related to them. These sequences — all tried and tested with children in schools — deal with poems individually and in groups and use a variety of techniques designed to help children to explore and respond to the poems. Each section concludes by suggesting other poems which might lend themselves to similar treatment.

Brian Merrick follows these practical activities with a more detailed discussion of the approaches and techniques used in them. Finally, there are extensive lists of poetry books that would be invaluable in the classroom and others related to poetry and poetry teaching.

(136 Pages Illustrated)

TALKING WITH CHARLES CAUSLEY

This booklet records a conversation in which the poet Charles Causley talks about his poetry and his 27 years as a primary school teacher in his home town of Launceston. There is an introduction by Brian Merrick, five poems by Charles Causley and a select bibliography for teachers. The booklet is illustrated by Charles Keeping.

(36 Pages Illustrated)

These titles are also available from NATE. See address opposite.

NATE

National Association for the Teaching of English

50 Broadfield Road, Broadfield Business Centre, Sheffield S8 0XJ
Telephone (0114) 255 5419   Fax (0114) 255 5296

NATE MEMBERSHIP PROVIDES:
★ An Information Service.
★ An Active Network of teachers sharing good practice.
★ A Quality Journal, "English in Education", three times a year.
★ A Full Subscription to "English Magazine" and/or "Primary English Magazine".
★ An Annual National Conference.
★ Regional Conferences and membership of your local branch.
★ Over 40 NATE Publications (with membership discounts).
★ Over 80 English Centre and other Publications.

If you are involved in the teaching of English and wish to keep informed you need to join us now!

Please send me membership details and catalogues.

NAME . . . .

ADDRESS . . . .

. . . .

. . . .
(Send this form to NATE Office at above address)

When the level of
enthusiasm is low
it may be time
to move on.